Driving Change

General Motors' Bold Leap Into The Electric Vehicle Revolution

Pauline R. Valerie

Copyright © 2024 Pauline R. Valerie

All rights reserved. No part of this publication may be reproduced, distributed, or transmitted in any form or by any means, including photocopying, recording, or other electronic or mechanical methods, without the prior written permission of the publisher, except in the case of brief quotations embodied in critical reviews and certain other noncommercial uses permitted by copyright law.

Table Of Contents

Introduction

Chapter One; Overview of GM's EV Strategy

Chapter Two; The Decision to Drop the 'Ultium' Name

Chapter Three; Production Goals for Electric Vehicles

Chapter Four; Financial Performance and Profitability

Chapter Five; Diversification of Battery Chemistries

Chapter Six; Impact of Market Conditions on EV Adoption

Chapter Seven; Changes in Leadership and Strategy

Chapter Eight; Sales Performance and Market Share

Chapter Nine; Revised Production Targets

Chapter Ten; Transition to Multi-Chemistry Battery Strategy

Chapter Eleven; Marketing and Advertising Efforts

Chapter Twelve; Rethinking Manufacturing and Production Facilities

Chapter Thirteen; Lessons Learned and Future Directions

Chapter Fourteen; Current and Future EV Production Plants

Conclusion

Introduction

In an era where the roar of engines is giving way to the silent hum of electric motors, the automotive industry stands at a crossroads. Picture a world where the air is cleaner, the streets are quieter, and the vehicles we drive not only serve our needs but also respect the planet we call home.

This vision is no longer a distant dream; it is rapidly becoming a reality, and General Motors (GM) is leading the charge. As one of the oldest and most storied names in automotive history, GM is embarking on a bold transformation, redefining its legacy for a new generation. The shift to electric vehicles (EVs) is not merely a change in product offerings; it represents a fundamental shift in the company's culture, operations, and strategic vision.

This book delves into the heart of GM's electric vehicle strategy, exploring the innovative steps the company is taking to adapt to a rapidly evolving market.

From the recent decision to retire the "Ultium" name—once heralded as a revolutionary breakthrough—to ambitious production goals and the diversification of battery technologies, GM's journey is one of resilience and reinvention. This narrative unfolds against a backdrop of shifting consumer preferences and competitive pressures, as the automotive landscape transforms before our eyes.

In the chapters that follow, we will examine the driving forces behind GM's strategic decisions, the challenges it faces in the ever-competitive EV market, and the remarkable achievements that mark its progress.

We'll explore how GM is embracing a multi-chemistry battery strategy, rethinking manufacturing and production facilities, and setting revised production targets to keep pace with consumer demand. Each chapter offers a unique lens through which to view the company's evolution and the broader implications for the automotive industry. As you turn these pages, you'll discover how GM is not just responding to the changing tides of the industry, but actively shaping the future of mobility.

Join us as we embark on this journey through the electric revolution, witnessing how a legacy brand is reinventing itself for a sustainable tomorrow, and uncovering the lessons learned along the way. Welcome to the future of General Motors—buckle up for an exciting ride.

Chapter One; Overview of GM's EV Strategy

General Motors (GM) is undergoing a significant transformation as it pivots toward an electric future. This shift is not merely a response to market trends; it reflects a deep commitment to sustainability and innovation that seeks to redefine the automotive landscape.

As the automotive industry grapples with the realities of climate change and consumer demand for cleaner energy, GM's electric vehicle (EV) strategy is evolving to meet these challenges head-on. For decades, GM has been a stalwart of the American automotive industry, known for its robust lineup of internal combustion engine vehicles. However, with increasing regulatory pressures and a growing societal push for greener alternatives, the company recognizes that the future lies in electrification.

This is not just a business decision; it's a fundamental shift in how GM envisions its role in a rapidly changing world. The company's ambitious goal is to eliminate tailpipe emissions from new light-duty vehicles by 2035, a commitment that underscores its dedication to sustainability.

One of the key elements of GM's EV strategy is the development and deployment of its proprietary Ultium battery technology. Initially launched with great fanfare, the Ultium platform was positioned as a revolutionary step forward in battery design, offering flexibility and efficiency. It enabled the production of a diverse range of vehicles, from mass-market models to high-performance electric cars.

However, the recent decision to move away from the "Ultium" branding signifies a broader reevaluation of the company's approach to battery technology and a commitment to embracing multiple battery chemistries and suppliers.

This pivot comes at a time when GM is ramping up its production capacity. The company has set an ambitious target to produce and sell approximately 200,000 EVs in North America by the end of the year, a substantial increase from previous years. While this number may seem modest compared to other industry players, it represents a significant milestone for GM as it strives to establish itself as a leader in the electric vehicle market. The shift to a dual strategy of manufacturing both traditional internal combustion engine vehicles and EVs allows GM to remain agile and responsive to market demands.

At the heart of GM's strategy is a commitment to reducing battery costs. Executives have emphasized that lowering the overall cost of EV batteries is critical to making electric vehicles more accessible to consumers.

This focus is not only about enhancing profit margins but also about ensuring that EVs can compete with their gasoline-powered counterparts on price. By optimizing production processes and diversifying battery types, GM aims to deliver quality vehicles that meet the needs of a broader customer base. Furthermore, GM is keenly aware of the challenges posed by slower-than-expected EV adoption rates.

The company has observed that, despite increasing sales—evidenced by a remarkable 60% year-over-year increase in EV sales in the third quarter—electric vehicles still account for only a small fraction of total sales.

This realization has prompted GM to rethink its marketing strategies and production timelines, ensuring that it aligns its offerings with customer demands. A pivotal aspect of GM's EV strategy is its willingness to learn from experience. The company has not shied away from acknowledging the need for adaptability in its operations. The leadership changes at GM, including the hiring of industry veterans from companies like Tesla, have infused fresh perspectives into the company's approach.

This influx of new talent has allowed GM to embrace innovative practices and rethink its production strategies, ensuring that it remains competitive in a crowded marketplace. Moreover, GM's commitment to a multi-chemistry battery strategy represents a significant shift in its operational framework.

Moving away from a single-source, single-chemistry model enables the company to tailor battery solutions to specific vehicle needs, optimizing performance and cost-efficiency. This strategy also diversifies supply chains, reducing reliance on any single supplier and mitigating risks associated with fluctuations in battery material costs. The company's plans extend beyond production numbers; they encompass the establishment of new production facilities designed specifically for electric vehicle manufacturing.

While the initial vision for a second all-electric vehicle plant in Orion Township has been delayed, this pause provides GM with an opportunity to reassess its strategies and align them with market realities.

It reflects a broader trend within the automotive industry, where flexibility and adaptability are essential in navigating the complexities of EV production. As GM moves forward, the overarching theme of its EV strategy is a blend of ambition and pragmatism. The journey towards a sustainable future is fraught with challenges, but GM is committed to evolving its practices and embracing innovation at every turn.

By fostering a culture of learning and responsiveness, GM aims to not only meet customer expectations but also lead the charge in the global transition to electric mobility.

In essence, GM's electric vehicle strategy is more than just a business model; it is a reflection of the company's dedication to creating a sustainable and innovative future. As it continues to adapt and grow, GM is poised to play a significant role in shaping the landscape of electric mobility for years to come.

Chapter Two; The Decision to Drop the 'Ultium' Name

The decision by General Motors (GM) to drop the "Ultium" name from its electric vehicle (EV) batteries and supporting technologies marks a pivotal moment in the company's journey toward electrification.

For years, "Ultium" has been synonymous with GM's ambitious plans for electric vehicles, symbolizing innovation and a new era in automotive design. However, as the landscape of the EV market continues to evolve, so too must GM's branding strategy. When GM first introduced the Ultium platform, it was heralded as a groundbreaking development that would revolutionize battery technology.

The Ultium batteries were designed to be versatile, enabling the production of a wide range of vehicles, from mass-market models to high-performance electric cars. The excitement surrounding the Ultium name was palpable; it was a bold declaration that GM was serious about leading the charge in the electric vehicle space.

But as the company moved forward, it became clear that the name had become a limiting factor rather than a stepping stone. The decision to retire the Ultium name was not made lightly. It reflects a deeper understanding of the rapidly changing market dynamics and the need for greater flexibility. GM has recognized that the electric vehicle landscape is increasingly competitive, with new players emerging and established companies pivoting to meet consumer demands.

In such a fast-paced environment, a single name tied to a singular battery technology can hinder innovation and limit options. By shedding the Ultium branding, GM is signaling a broader commitment to diversify its battery offerings and embrace a multi-chemistry, multi-supplier approach.

This shift is particularly relevant as GM grapples with the realities of electric vehicle adoption. Despite the significant investments made in developing the Ultium platform, EV sales have not surged as anticipated. In the third quarter, GM reported a 60% increase in electric vehicle sales year-over-year, yet these numbers still represent a small fraction of the company's overall sales.

The realization that consumer uptake has been slower than expected prompted a reevaluation of not just the technology but also the branding that encapsulates it. Moreover, the move away from the Ultium name allows GM to take a fresh look at its battery strategy without being tethered to the expectations set by that original branding.

Executives have acknowledged that the automotive market is shifting toward a more nuanced understanding of battery technology. The days of a one-size-fits-all approach are waning, and the industry is moving toward a model that embraces multiple types of batteries, each optimized for specific vehicle needs. This strategic pivot reflects GM's recognition that consumers desire variety and choice in their electric vehicles.

This transition is also an acknowledgment of the lessons learned from the past. GM has invested billions in the development of Ultium technologies and marketing efforts that aimed to position the brand as a leader in the electric vehicle space.

Yet, as the company reevaluates its trajectory, it understands the importance of adapting to market conditions. The influx of new leadership, including veterans from Tesla, has infused GM with fresh perspectives on what it means to be competitive in this evolving landscape. The decision to drop the Ultium name is not just about rebranding; it is also about restoring consumer confidence and enhancing GM's ability to respond to the needs of the market.

As consumers become more discerning about their choices, they are looking for transparency and variety in the products they purchase. By moving away from a single branding strategy, GM can better align itself with consumer expectations, offering a wider array of vehicles powered by different battery technologies.

This flexibility could be the key to unlocking greater market share and ensuring the company remains relevant in an increasingly electrified world. Additionally, GM's commitment to a multi-chemistry battery strategy signifies a departure from its initial approach and an embrace of a more collaborative ecosystem. This decision allows the company to work with various suppliers and innovators, leveraging their expertise to create the best possible products.

Such collaboration not only diversifies GM's offerings but also mitigates risks associated with supply chain disruptions, which have become increasingly prominent in recent years. Ultimately, the decision to drop the Ultium name is a reflection of GM's broader strategy to adapt, innovate, and thrive in an unpredictable market.

It is a bold move that demonstrates the company's willingness to learn from the past while setting its sights on the future. As GM continues to redefine its electric vehicle strategy, this decision stands as a testament to its commitment to not only keeping pace with industry changes but also leading the charge in creating a sustainable and diverse automotive landscape. In addition, the retirement of the Ultium name is more than a simple rebranding; it represents GM's evolution in the face of market realities.

As the company embraces new strategies and technologies, it is poised to carve out a significant presence in the electric vehicle market, ensuring that it remains a key player in the automotive industry for years to come.

Chapter Three; Production Goals for Electric Vehicles

As General Motors (GM) charts its course in the electric vehicle (EV) landscape, the company's production goals represent not just numbers on a page but a vision for a sustainable future.

With a target of producing approximately 200,000 EVs for North America by the end of the year, GM is making a bold statement about its commitment to electrification. This ambitious goal is underpinned by a strategic focus on enhancing production capabilities, streamlining operations, and responding to consumer demands in a rapidly changing market. The automotive industry is experiencing a seismic shift, with electric vehicles moving from niche products to mainstream options.

As consumers become more environmentally conscious and governments enforce stricter emissions regulations, GM recognizes the urgency of scaling its production to meet these new demands.

The company's goal of 200,000 EVs is not just a response to market trends; it is a reflection of a larger commitment to sustainability and innovation. It's a chance for GM to showcase its prowess as a leader in the automotive industry, emphasizing the potential of electric vehicles to shape a cleaner, greener future. Achieving this production goal requires significant operational changes and investments.

GM has been proactive in establishing new manufacturing processes and technologies to support its electric vehicle initiatives. One notable aspect of this effort is the construction of dedicated EV production facilities, such as Factory Zero in Detroit, which is designed exclusively for electric vehicle assembly.

This plant symbolizes GM's commitment to innovation, as it integrates advanced manufacturing techniques to streamline production and improve efficiency. Factory Zero serves as a model for future facilities, emphasizing that the shift to electric vehicles is not merely a change in the product but a transformation of the entire production ecosystem. In addition to expanding its manufacturing footprint, GM is also focusing on diversifying its supply chain to enhance production capabilities.

The decision to move away from the Ultium name signals a broader approach to battery technology, allowing GM to leverage multiple suppliers and chemistries. This flexibility not only enhances the company's ability to produce various EV models but also mitigates risks associated with supply chain disruptions.

By embracing a multi-supplier strategy, GM can ensure a steady supply of essential components, ultimately supporting its ambitious production goals. The timeline for achieving these production targets is critical. GM CEO Mary Barra has emphasized the importance of speed and efficiency in ramping up EV production. The company aims to achieve profitability on a contribution-margin basis by the end of the year, a milestone that underscores the commitment to not only producing vehicles but also ensuring they are financially viable.

This emphasis on profitability is essential in a competitive market where automakers are vying for consumer attention and market share. Consumer demand is another driving force behind GM's production goals.

The company is acutely aware that the electric vehicle market is not monolithic; it is diverse, with consumers seeking different features, styles, and price points. As such, GM is committed to producing a wide range of electric vehicles that cater to various segments of the market. From compact models to SUVs and trucks, GM's strategy involves offering options that appeal to a broad audience. This understanding of consumer preferences is crucial as the company works to establish itself as a leading player in the electric vehicle space.

However, reaching the production target of 200,000 EVs is not without challenges. The automotive industry is facing hurdles such as supply chain constraints, fluctuating raw material costs, and the need for skilled labor in EV production.

GM is actively addressing these issues by investing in workforce development and fostering partnerships with suppliers. This holistic approach ensures that the company is not only focused on numbers but also on the people and processes that make those numbers possible. Moreover, GM's production goals are intricately linked to the company's broader sustainability objectives. As GM aims for carbon neutrality by 2040, the production of electric vehicles is a crucial step toward achieving this vision.

Each vehicle produced contributes to a reduction in greenhouse gas emissions, aligning with global efforts to combat climate change. This commitment to sustainability resonates with consumers, who are increasingly prioritizing environmentally friendly options in their purchasing decisions.

As GM advances toward its production targets, the company is also keenly aware of the importance of transparency and communication. Engaging with consumers, stakeholders, and the community is vital to building trust and ensuring that the company's goals align with public expectations. GM's willingness to share its progress, challenges, and successes fosters a sense of collaboration and shared purpose in the journey toward electrification.

Moreover, GM's production goals for electric vehicles encapsulate a broader vision for the future of mobility. By setting ambitious targets, investing in innovative manufacturing processes, and embracing a diverse range of battery technologies, GM is positioning itself as a leader in the electric vehicle market.

As the company navigates the challenges and opportunities of this transformative period, its commitment to sustainability and consumer engagement will be crucial in shaping the next chapter of the automotive industry. The road ahead may be complex, but GM is determined to drive forward, making its mark in the world of electric vehicles and contributing to a cleaner, greener planet.

Chapter Four; Financial Performance and Profitability

As General Motors (GM) embarks on its electric vehicle (EV) journey, financial performance and profitability have taken center stage in discussions about the company's future.

The shift to electric vehicles is not just a matter of innovation; it's also a financial imperative. For GM, navigating this transition means balancing the need for substantial investments in technology and infrastructure with the goal of achieving sustainable profitability. In recent years, GM has made significant strides in its financial performance, reflecting a commitment to adapt to the evolving automotive landscape.

The company has announced plans to produce around 200,000 EVs for North America this year, a bold target that indicates confidence in both consumer demand and the company's ability to deliver. Achieving this production goal is crucial not only for market positioning but also for enhancing GM's bottom line.

The potential profitability associated with electric vehicle sales has garnered attention from investors and stakeholders, who are eager to see how the company can capitalize on this growing segment. Financial health is about more than just sales numbers; it encompasses a comprehensive approach to managing costs, investments, and revenues. GM has recognized the need to lower battery costs as a critical factor in making electric vehicles competitive with traditional internal combustion engine vehicles.

The company has invested heavily in developing its battery technology, which is essential for reducing production costs and increasing profit margins. By optimizing battery design and production methods, GM aims to create EVs that not only appeal to environmentally conscious consumers but also fit within their budgets.

In addition to cutting costs, GM is actively pursuing partnerships and collaborations to bolster its financial performance. The decision to embrace a multi-supplier strategy for batteries allows GM to source materials from various vendors, reducing reliance on a single source and mitigating risks associated with supply chain disruptions. This strategy not only helps control costs but also enhances the flexibility needed to respond to changing market conditions.

By fostering relationships with key players in the battery and EV space, GM is positioning itself for long-term success while maintaining a keen focus on profitability. The automotive industry is often cyclical, with periods of growth and contraction influenced by economic factors and consumer behavior.

GM's leadership is acutely aware of these dynamics and has taken steps to ensure the company remains resilient during challenging times. For example, while the company aims for profitability on a contribution-margin basis by the end of the year, it is also preparing for potential economic downturns that could impact consumer spending. By maintaining a diverse portfolio of vehicles, including traditional gas-powered cars and trucks alongside EVs, GM can mitigate risks and capitalize on varying consumer preferences.

Another key factor influencing GM's financial performance is its commitment to sustainability. As the world moves toward stricter emissions regulations, the demand for electric vehicles is expected to grow.

By investing in EV production and technology, GM is not only aligning itself with environmental goals but also positioning itself to capture a significant share of the burgeoning market. This foresight is critical for ensuring long-term profitability, as consumers increasingly gravitate toward brands that prioritize sustainability and environmental responsibility. Furthermore, GM's financial performance is bolstered by its ability to innovate continuously.

The company is exploring various avenues to enhance its product offerings and improve operational efficiency. From integrating advanced manufacturing techniques to leveraging data analytics for better decision-making, GM is committed to staying ahead of the curve.

This focus on innovation not only drives revenue growth but also fosters a culture of creativity within the organization, ultimately contributing to improved profitability. As GM continues to invest in electric vehicles, it is also essential for the company to maintain transparency with its stakeholders. Clear communication about financial performance, production goals, and the challenges faced in transitioning to electric vehicles is crucial for building trust and confidence.

By engaging openly with investors, consumers, and the broader community, GM can create a narrative that highlights its commitment to profitability while navigating the complexities of the automotive market.

In recent quarters, GM has reported positive trends in its financial performance, with increasing sales figures and improved margins in its traditional vehicle segments. However, the transition to electric vehicles presents both opportunities and challenges. As the company ramps up production of EVs, it will be critical to monitor costs closely, ensuring that investments translate into tangible returns. This requires not only effective management of resources but also a keen understanding of market dynamics and consumer preferences.

However, GM's financial performance and profitability are intricately linked to its strategy for electric vehicles. By focusing on reducing costs, fostering partnerships, and committing to sustainability, the company is positioning itself for success in a rapidly changing market.

While challenges lie ahead, GM's proactive approach and commitment to innovation signal a promising future. As the company navigates this transformative period, its ability to balance investment with profitability will be key to solidifying its status as a leader in the electric vehicle industry, ultimately shaping the future of transportation for generations to come.

Chapter Five; Diversification of Battery Chemistries

As General Motors (GM) continues to forge ahead in the electric vehicle (EV) landscape, one of the key strategies shaping its future is the diversification of battery chemistries.

This approach marks a significant shift in how the company thinks about energy storage and vehicle performance, reflecting a deeper understanding of the evolving demands of the automotive market. By embracing a broader range of battery technologies, GM aims to enhance the efficiency, performance, and overall appeal of its electric vehicles. At the heart of this diversification is the recognition that no single battery chemistry will suit every application.

Different vehicles have different requirements in terms of range, power, and cost. For example, a compact electric vehicle may prioritize affordability and efficiency, while a high-performance sports car might demand a battery that delivers maximum power and rapid charging capabilities.

By exploring various chemistries, GM is positioning itself to meet the diverse needs of consumers while optimizing the performance of its vehicles. Historically, GM has relied heavily on lithium-ion batteries, which have become the industry standard due to their energy density and relatively low cost. However, as the market matures, the limitations of this technology have become increasingly apparent. Lithium-ion batteries can be expensive to produce, and their performance can degrade over time.

Additionally, the supply of critical materials, such as lithium and cobalt, is subject to market fluctuations and geopolitical factors that can impact availability and pricing.

Recognizing these challenges, GM has set out to explore alternative battery chemistries that could offer better performance, reduced costs, and greater sustainability. One promising avenue for diversification is the development of solid-state batteries. Unlike traditional lithium-ion batteries that use liquid electrolytes, solid-state batteries utilize solid electrolytes, which can significantly enhance safety and energy density.

These batteries are less prone to overheating and are generally more stable, making them an attractive option for high-performance applications. GM's exploration of solid-state technology could lead to vehicles with longer ranges and faster charging times, addressing two of the most significant consumer concerns in the EV market.

In addition to solid-state batteries, GM is also investigating other chemistries, such as lithium iron phosphate (LFP) and nickel-manganese-cobalt (NMC) formulations. LFP batteries, for example, are known for their thermal stability and longevity, making them an excellent choice for applications where safety and durability are paramount. They are often less expensive to produce than traditional lithium-ion batteries, which can translate into lower vehicle prices for consumers.

By incorporating LFP technology into its lineup, GM can cater to budget-conscious buyers without compromising on quality. The decision to diversify battery chemistries is also rooted in GM's commitment to sustainability.

As the company aims for carbon neutrality by 2040, it understands that the materials used in battery production can significantly impact its overall environmental footprint. By exploring alternative chemistries and sourcing materials responsibly, GM can minimize the ecological impact of its vehicles while promoting a more circular economy. This focus on sustainability resonates with consumers, particularly younger buyers who prioritize environmental responsibility in their purchasing decisions.

To support its diversification strategy, GM is not only investing in research and development but also building strong partnerships with leading battery suppliers and technology companies.

Collaborations with firms like LG Energy Solution and Samsung SDI demonstrate GM's commitment to leveraging external expertise while fostering innovation. By engaging with these partners, GM can tap into a wealth of knowledge and resources, accelerating the development of new battery technologies that can be integrated into its electric vehicles. Furthermore, GM's commitment to diversification reflects a broader trend within the automotive industry.

As more manufacturers enter the electric vehicle market, the competition will intensify. Companies that rely solely on traditional lithium-ion batteries may find themselves at a disadvantage as consumer preferences shift and new technologies emerge.

By positioning itself at the forefront of battery innovation, GM can maintain its competitive edge and adapt to the changing landscape of the automotive market. The diversification of battery chemistries is not just a technical endeavor; it also represents a cultural shift within GM. The company is fostering a mindset of innovation and adaptability, encouraging its teams to think creatively about the future of electric vehicles.

This cultural transformation is crucial as GM navigates the complexities of the EV market and strives to meet the demands of an increasingly discerning consumer base.

Ultimately, GM's strategy of diversifying battery chemistries is a testament to its commitment to innovation, sustainability, and consumer satisfaction. By exploring various technologies, from solid-state batteries to lithium iron phosphate, GM is positioning itself to meet the diverse needs of the electric vehicle market. This proactive approach not only enhances vehicle performance and affordability but also aligns with the company's broader sustainability goals.

As GM continues to lead the charge in the electrification of transportation, its commitment to battery diversification will play a pivotal role in shaping the future of the automotive industry, ensuring that it remains at the forefront of innovation for years to come.

Chapter Six; Impact of Market Conditions on EV Adoption

The adoption of electric vehicles (EVs) has been one of the most discussed topics in the automotive industry in recent years. As we stand at the crossroads of a transformative era in transportation, it's essential to recognize how market conditions influence the pace and extent of EV adoption.

A confluence of factors, including economic trends, technological advancements, consumer sentiment, and government policies, shape the landscape in which electric vehicles are either embraced or hesitated upon. One of the most significant market conditions impacting EV adoption is the cost of vehicles and the availability of financing options.

Historically, electric vehicles have carried a premium price tag compared to their gasoline-powered counterparts. Although prices for EVs have been decreasing due to advancements in battery technology and economies of scale, the initial investment remains a barrier for many potential buyers.

As consumers weigh their options, financing opportunities play a crucial role. Attractive lease and loan terms can make EVs more accessible, allowing a wider audience to consider the switch. Conversely, if interest rates rise or economic uncertainty looms, potential buyers may hesitate to invest in a new vehicle, regardless of its electric capabilities. In tandem with pricing, the fluctuating cost of fuel influences consumer decisions. Rising gasoline prices often correlate with increased interest in electric vehicles.

When consumers feel the pinch at the pump, the allure of a vehicle powered by electricity becomes more pronounced. The operating cost savings associated with EVs can provide a compelling incentive, especially for those who drive significant distances.

This relationship between fuel prices and EV adoption illustrates how market conditions can shift consumer priorities and preferences in real-time. Another crucial factor is the availability and development of charging infrastructure. For many potential EV owners, the "range anxiety" associated with running out of battery on long trips can be a daunting concern. The expansion of charging networks is vital to alleviate these fears and make electric vehicle ownership more feasible.

In areas where charging stations are plentiful and conveniently located, consumers are more likely to consider an electric vehicle. Conversely, in regions lacking adequate infrastructure, potential buyers may feel deterred.

GM and other automakers recognize this challenge, actively investing in charging solutions and working with governments and private companies to enhance the availability of charging stations. Consumer awareness and education also play a pivotal role in the adoption of electric vehicles. As electric vehicles become more mainstream, there is an increasing need to inform potential buyers about the benefits and practicalities of EV ownership.

Many consumers remain unaware of the total cost of ownership advantages of EVs, including lower maintenance costs and available incentives. Dealerships and automakers must take on the responsibility of educating their sales teams and customers alike, highlighting the advantages of electric vehicles and addressing common misconceptions.

As knowledge grows, so too does the likelihood of adoption. The impact of government policies and incentives cannot be overstated. Many countries and states have implemented programs designed to encourage the adoption of electric vehicles, offering tax credits, rebates, and other financial incentives. These policies can significantly influence consumer behavior, making EVs more affordable and appealing.

However, these incentives can also be subject to change based on political landscapes, which creates an element of uncertainty. For example, shifts in administration can lead to new policies that either bolster or diminish support for electric vehicles. The inconsistency of such programs can make it challenging for consumers to feel confident in their purchasing decisions.

In addition to economic factors, the cultural context surrounding electric vehicles also plays a significant role in adoption rates. Societal attitudes towards sustainability and environmental responsibility are becoming increasingly prevalent, particularly among younger generations. As climate change concerns grow, many consumers are seeking ways to reduce their carbon footprints, making electric vehicles an attractive option. However, cultural resistance can still be a barrier.

In regions where traditional vehicles are deeply embedded in local identity and lifestyle, changing perceptions and behaviors takes time. Community engagement and grassroots movements can help bridge this gap, fostering a more welcoming environment for electric vehicles.

The global pandemic has also left its mark on the automotive industry and EV adoption. While initial lockdowns caused a temporary dip in vehicle sales, the subsequent recovery has brought new opportunities. Remote work and changing commuting patterns have prompted many individuals to reevaluate their transportation needs. As people spend more time at home, the appeal of an electric vehicle—especially one that can be charged overnight in the garage—grows.

Additionally, the pandemic has accelerated interest in health and sustainability, leading many to seek cleaner alternatives to traditional vehicles. Moreso, the impact of market conditions on electric vehicle adoption is multifaceted and ever-evolving.

Economic factors, consumer sentiment, technological advancements, infrastructure development, and government policies all intertwine to create a complex landscape for EVs. As General Motors and other automakers navigate these challenges, understanding the nuances of market dynamics will be critical for shaping the future of transportation. By addressing barriers, educating consumers, and investing in infrastructure, the automotive industry can help usher in a new era of electric mobility—one that promises not only sustainability but also a redefined relationship between individuals and their vehicles.

As we move forward, the potential for electric vehicles to transform our roads and communities remains bright, provided that the industry can adapt and respond to the evolving marketplace.

Chapter Seven; Changes in Leadership and Strategy

As the automotive landscape undergoes rapid transformation, companies like General Motors (GM) are recognizing the need for agile leadership and strategic pivots to stay relevant in an increasingly competitive market.

The transition to electric vehicles (EVs) has prompted GM to reevaluate not only its product offerings but also its leadership structure and overall strategy. This evolution is not just about adapting to new technologies; it's about redefining the very essence of the company to meet the demands of a changing world. In recent years, GM has seen a shift in leadership that reflects its commitment to embracing innovation and sustainability.

The company has brought in executives with diverse backgrounds and experiences, including veterans from technology and other industries. This influx of fresh perspectives is vital as GM navigates the complexities of the EV market, which requires not just automotive expertise but also a deep understanding of software, data analytics, and consumer behavior.

By blending traditional automotive knowledge with new-age thinking, GM is positioning itself to tackle the challenges of tomorrow head-on. One notable change in leadership was the appointment of key figures from Tesla and other tech companies. These leaders come equipped with a wealth of experience in EV manufacturing and development, as well as insights into the fast-paced world of technology.

Their presence signifies a strategic shift in GM's approach to electric vehicle production, emphasizing innovation, speed, and adaptability. By integrating these leaders into its ranks, GM is making a statement: it recognizes that to thrive in this new era, it must think like a tech company while remaining rooted in its automotive heritage.

This leadership transformation is accompanied by a comprehensive strategy aimed at redefining GM's vision for the future. The company has set ambitious goals to become a leader in the electric vehicle space, with plans to invest billions of dollars in EV development and production. This commitment goes beyond merely introducing new models; it encompasses the entire ecosystem of electric vehicles, including battery technology, charging infrastructure, and sustainable manufacturing processes.

By adopting a holistic approach, GM aims to ensure that its electric vehicles are not only technologically advanced but also economically viable and environmentally friendly. Part of this strategic overhaul includes a renewed focus on customer needs and preferences.

Understanding the evolving expectations of consumers is essential in an era where sustainability is paramount. GM recognizes that today's buyers are not just looking for a means of transportation; they want a vehicle that aligns with their values and lifestyle. To this end, the company is investing in research and development to create electric vehicles that offer enhanced performance, longer ranges, and advanced features, all while maintaining affordability. This consumer-centric approach is a departure from the past and signals a commitment to truly meeting the demands of the market.

In addition to changes in leadership and strategy, GM is also rethinking its organizational structure to foster collaboration and innovation. The company is breaking down silos and encouraging cross-functional teams to work together in developing electric vehicles.

This shift in culture promotes the exchange of ideas and accelerates problem-solving, ensuring that GM can respond quickly to market demands and technological advancements. By fostering an environment of collaboration, GM is positioning itself to be nimble and responsive in an ever-changing landscape. Moreover, GM's commitment to sustainability is a driving force behind its strategic initiatives. The company has set a goal to achieve carbon neutrality by 2040, a bold ambition that reflects a broader industry trend toward environmentally responsible practices.

This commitment to sustainability is not just about compliance with regulations; it's about creating a legacy that resonates with consumers. By prioritizing sustainable practices across its operations—from sourcing materials to manufacturing processes—GM aims to set itself apart in the crowded automotive market.

While the journey toward a fully electric future is filled with challenges, GM's leadership is embracing these hurdles as opportunities for growth. The company is actively engaging with stakeholders, including consumers, policymakers, and industry partners, to shape the future of transportation. By collaborating with other entities, GM is leveraging collective expertise to address common challenges, such as developing charging infrastructure and advocating for supportive policies.

This collaborative approach underscores GM's commitment to being a responsible corporate citizen while driving innovation. The changes in leadership and strategy at GM are reflective of a broader shift within the automotive industry.

As electric vehicles gain traction, traditional automakers are reevaluating their positions and recognizing that the future of transportation is not solely about producing cars; it's about creating a sustainable ecosystem that benefits society as a whole. GM's strategic initiatives exemplify this understanding, as the company strives to not only lead in EV production but also to inspire a cultural shift toward sustainable mobility.

Furthermore, GM's changes in leadership and strategy are vital components of its journey toward becoming a leader in the electric vehicle market.

By embracing innovation, fostering collaboration, and prioritizing sustainability, the company is positioning itself for success in a rapidly evolving landscape. As GM continues to navigate the challenges and opportunities of the electric vehicle revolution, its leadership's vision and strategic direction will play a crucial role in shaping the future of transportation. With a focus on customer needs and a commitment to responsible practices, GM is not just adapting to change; it is actively shaping the future of mobility for generations to come.

Chapter Eight; Sales Performance and Market Share

The sales performance and market share of electric vehicles (EVs) have become pivotal metrics for automakers like General Motors (GM) as they navigate the rapidly changing automotive landscape.

As the world shifts toward more sustainable transportation solutions, understanding how GM fares in this new arena is crucial not only for the company but also for the consumers and investors who are watching closely. In recent years, GM has committed to electrifying its lineup, aiming to transition from a traditional automaker to a leader in the electric vehicle space.

This ambitious strategy is part of a broader vision to reshape the company's future, driven by both market demand for greener alternatives and an urgent need to address climate change. As part of this transition, GM has set concrete sales targets and market share goals that reflect its aspirations in the EV segment.

Sales performance is a critical indicator of how well GM is executing its electric vehicle strategy. Recent figures show that GM has seen a notable uptick in EV sales, reporting a 60% year-over-year increase in the third quarter. This surge translates to roughly 32,100 electric vehicles sold, a significant step in establishing a foothold in a market that is still in its infancy. However, despite this positive momentum, EVs accounted for only about 4.9% of GM's total sales during this period, highlighting the challenges that remain in capturing a larger share of the market.

One of the primary hurdles GM faces is the intense competition from both established automotive players and new entrants in the EV market. Companies like Tesla have set the benchmark for electric vehicle sales and innovation, and other traditional automakers are also ramping up their efforts to catch up.

The pressure is on for GM to differentiate itself and offer compelling reasons for consumers to choose its electric models over competitors'. This means that beyond just selling cars, GM must foster brand loyalty and build a reputation for quality, performance, and sustainability. Market share is another crucial aspect of GM's strategy as it navigates the competitive landscape of electric vehicles. GM's goal of producing approximately 200,000 EVs in North America this year reflects a strategic attempt to increase its market presence.

This target has been recalibrated from earlier estimates, which anticipated even higher production numbers. The reality is that the path to capturing market share in the electric vehicle segment is fraught with challenges, including supply chain disruptions and evolving consumer preferences.

To effectively increase its market share, GM is focusing on diversifying its EV offerings. The company is introducing a range of electric models that cater to different consumer needs, from affordable compact cars to luxury SUVs. This diversification strategy aims to appeal to a broader audience, ensuring that there is something for everyone in GM's electric vehicle lineup. By expanding its offerings, GM hopes to attract new customers while retaining existing ones who may be considering an electric vehicle for the first time.

Another critical component of GM's strategy is its commitment to investing in infrastructure and technology. Recognizing that the success of electric vehicles is tied to the availability of charging stations, GM is working to expand the charging network.

Collaborating with various partners, the company is aiming to make charging as convenient as filling up a tank with gasoline. This investment in infrastructure not only enhances the user experience but also helps alleviate range anxiety, a common concern among potential EV buyers. Furthermore, GM is capitalizing on partnerships and collaborations to boost its sales performance and market share. The company has formed strategic alliances with technology firms and energy providers to create a robust ecosystem around its electric vehicles.

These collaborations allow GM to tap into expertise that enhances its product offerings and marketing strategies, ultimately driving sales growth. Consumer education and awareness also play a significant role in shaping sales performance.

Many potential buyers may still be hesitant about switching to electric vehicles due to misconceptions or a lack of understanding about the benefits. GM recognizes this challenge and is actively working to inform consumers about the advantages of EVs, such as lower operating costs, reduced environmental impact, and government incentives. By promoting these benefits, GM hopes to inspire confidence in electric vehicle ownership and stimulate sales.

As GM navigates the complexities of the EV market, its sales performance will be closely monitored by investors and industry observers. The company's ability to meet its production targets, expand its market share, and build a loyal customer base will ultimately determine its success in the electric vehicle sector.

While the road ahead may be challenging, GM's commitment to innovation, sustainability, and consumer satisfaction positions it well to capitalize on the growing demand for electric vehicles. In summary, the sales performance and market share of GM in the electric vehicle market are critical components of its broader strategy to transition to a sustainable future. As the company works to increase its production, diversify its offerings, and invest in infrastructure, it remains focused on capturing a larger share of the growing EV market.

The interplay between competition, consumer preferences, and market dynamics will shape GM's trajectory in the coming years. Ultimately, by staying attuned to these factors and maintaining a commitment to quality and innovation, GM is well-positioned to thrive in the electric vehicle landscape and drive forward the future of transportation.

Chapter Nine; Revised Production Targets

As the electric vehicle (EV) market continues to evolve, automakers are increasingly faced with the necessity of setting and adjusting production targets that reflect both consumer demand and the rapidly changing landscape of the automotive industry.

General Motors (GM) is no exception. The company has been at the forefront of the transition to electric vehicles, and its revised production targets underscore its commitment to becoming a leader in this transformative sector. However, these targets are not merely numbers on a page; they represent a complex interplay of strategy, market conditions, and the quest for sustainable innovation.

In recent months, GM has recalibrated its production goals, acknowledging the challenges and opportunities inherent in the electric vehicle market. Originally aiming to produce up to 300,000 EVs, the company has adjusted its target to a more modest 200,000 to 250,000 units for the year.

This revision reflects a prudent approach to the realities of EV adoption, acknowledging that while consumer interest is growing, the pace of that growth is not as rapid as previously anticipated. This adjustment is not a retreat; rather, it demonstrates GM's willingness to be realistic and flexible in a dynamic market environment. One of the key factors influencing GM's revised production targets is the overall state of the electric vehicle market. While there is undeniable momentum toward electrification, the actual rate of adoption has been slower than many industry experts had predicted.

Consumers are still navigating the learning curve associated with electric vehicles, from understanding charging infrastructure to assessing the long-term value of ownership. GM's decision to lower its production goals acknowledges this complexity and reflects a strategic pivot to better align with consumer readiness and market demand.

Additionally, GM's production targets are influenced by its ongoing efforts to diversify battery chemistries and technologies. As the company moves away from its original Ultium pouch cell strategy, it is exploring multiple battery types and chemistries that could optimize performance for different vehicle models. This strategic shift requires time and resources, impacting production timelines. By revising its targets, GM is not only managing expectations but also ensuring that its vehicles meet the highest standards of efficiency and performance when they hit the market.

Another significant aspect of GM's revised production targets is the company's focus on profitability. In a highly competitive landscape, GM understands that it cannot afford to prioritize volume over the sustainability of its business model.

Achieving profitability in the electric vehicle segment is paramount, and the revised targets reflect a careful consideration of production costs, supply chain logistics, and overall market conditions. By setting more achievable goals, GM aims to optimize its resources and ensure that each vehicle produced contributes positively to its bottom line.

The announcement of revised production targets also highlights GM's adaptability in the face of changing market conditions. The automotive industry has seen substantial fluctuations in consumer preferences, regulatory requirements, and supply chain dynamics.

As the world grapples with issues like semiconductor shortages and raw material availability, GM's willingness to recalibrate its production goals demonstrates its responsiveness to external challenges. This agility is crucial in maintaining a competitive edge in an environment that demands quick decision-making and strategic foresight. Moreover, GM's commitment to investing in manufacturing capacity and infrastructure is integral to its revised production strategy.

The company is not only focused on meeting its current targets but is also laying the groundwork for future growth. By investing in new manufacturing facilities and enhancing existing plants, GM is positioning itself to ramp up production capabilities when market conditions become more favorable.

This forward-thinking approach reflects a long-term vision that goes beyond immediate production numbers. The human element behind GM's revised production targets cannot be overlooked. The shift in strategy is driven by a diverse team of executives, engineers, and innovators who are passionate about creating a sustainable future. Their collective insights and experiences shape the company's approach to electric vehicles, ensuring that decisions are informed by a deep understanding of consumer needs and market trends.

This commitment to collaboration and innovation fosters a culture of adaptability within GM, enabling it to navigate the complexities of the automotive landscape with confidence. As GM moves forward with its revised production targets, it remains steadfast in its mission to lead the charge toward electric mobility.

The company is actively engaging with consumers, stakeholders, and industry partners to promote the benefits of electric vehicles and address any concerns related to ownership. By building a strong connection with its audience, GM aims to inspire confidence in its products and foster a sense of community around the transition to electric mobility. In addition, GM's revised production targets signify a thoughtful and strategic response to the evolving landscape of electric vehicles.

By adjusting its goals in line with market realities, consumer readiness, and profitability objectives, GM demonstrates its commitment to sustainable growth and innovation.

These targets are not just about numbers; they represent a comprehensive strategy aimed at capturing market share while ensuring that the company remains resilient in the face of challenges. As GM continues to adapt and evolve, its focus on creating a robust and sustainable electric vehicle ecosystem will be crucial in shaping the future of transportation for generations to come.

Chapter Ten; Transition to Multi-Chemistry Battery Strategy

As the automotive industry shifts toward electric vehicles (EVs), the technology behind their power sources is evolving just as rapidly. General Motors (GM) is at the forefront of this transition, particularly with its strategic move toward a multi-chemistry battery approach.

This pivot signifies more than just a change in materials; it embodies a comprehensive strategy aimed at optimizing performance, reducing costs, and ensuring sustainability in the rapidly changing electric vehicle landscape. Traditionally, many automakers, including GM, relied heavily on a single type of battery chemistry—specifically, lithium-ion batteries with nickel manganese cobalt (NMC) formulations.

While these batteries have been effective, the growing demand for electric vehicles has prompted GM to reconsider this singular focus. The transition to a multi-chemistry battery strategy is a recognition that different vehicle types and applications require tailored solutions to meet diverse performance and cost goals.

One of the most compelling reasons for this transition is the need for flexibility in battery production. By diversifying the chemistries used in its electric vehicles, GM can optimize each battery type for specific applications, whether it's a compact car, an SUV, or a high-performance vehicle. For instance, GM might use prismatic cells, which are known for their efficiency and compact design, for certain models, while employing other chemistries that might be better suited for larger, more powerful vehicles.

This tailored approach allows GM to enhance the driving experience across its lineup while also catering to a wider range of consumer needs. Moreover, a multi-chemistry strategy helps GM address the ongoing challenges of supply chain management.

The electric vehicle market is facing shortages in critical materials like lithium, cobalt, and nickel. By broadening its battery chemistry portfolio, GM can reduce its dependence on these scarce resources. This diversification not only mitigates supply chain risks but also opens up opportunities for innovation in sourcing and production. For example, GM is exploring partnerships with battery suppliers that can provide alternative materials or chemistries, further securing its position in the market.

Environmental sustainability is another crucial aspect of GM's shift to a multi-chemistry battery strategy. As consumers become more environmentally conscious, automakers are under increasing pressure to produce greener products.

By leveraging a variety of battery chemistries, GM can improve the recyclability of its batteries and reduce the overall environmental impact of its electric vehicles. Additionally, using alternative materials can lead to less intensive mining practices and a smaller carbon footprint throughout the battery life cycle. While the benefits of a multi-chemistry strategy are clear, transitioning from a single-chemistry approach presents its own challenges.

Integrating different battery technologies requires substantial investment in research and development, manufacturing capabilities, and staff training. GM is investing heavily in these areas, ensuring that its workforce is equipped with the necessary skills to handle a diverse range of battery technologies.

This investment in human capital is crucial for fostering a culture of innovation and adaptability within the organization. Consumer perception also plays a vital role in the success of GM's multi-chemistry strategy. Many potential EV buyers still hold reservations about the reliability and performance of electric vehicles, often stemming from past experiences with battery technology. GM understands that to win over consumers, it must not only deliver high-quality vehicles but also effectively communicate the advantages of its diverse battery offerings.

This means engaging in transparent conversations about the performance, safety, and longevity of different battery chemistries. By fostering trust and confidence in its technology, GM aims to dispel myths and highlight the benefits of its innovative approach.

As GM embarks on this transition, it is also actively collaborating with external partners and industry leaders. This collaborative spirit is essential for staying ahead of technological advancements and regulatory requirements. By joining forces with academic institutions, research organizations, and other automakers, GM can leverage a broader knowledge base and accelerate the development of new battery technologies.

These partnerships will be instrumental in navigating the complexities of the battery landscape and ensuring that GM remains a leader in the electric vehicle market. GM's transition to a multi-chemistry battery strategy represents a forward-thinking approach to electric vehicle development.

By diversifying its battery technologies, GM is not only enhancing its product offerings but also addressing key challenges related to supply chain management, sustainability, and consumer perception. This strategic pivot is about more than just keeping pace with industry trends; it reflects a deep commitment to innovation, quality, and the future of transportation. As GM continues to explore and implement this multifaceted battery strategy, it is positioning itself to thrive in the evolving landscape of electric mobility, ultimately benefiting consumers and the planet alike.

The road ahead is undoubtedly challenging, but GM's proactive approach and dedication to adaptability are paving the way for a more sustainable and electrifying future.

Chapter Eleven; Marketing and Advertising Efforts

In an era where electric vehicles (EVs) are gaining momentum and reshaping the automotive landscape, General Motors (GM) has embarked on a journey to redefine how it markets and advertises its innovative offerings.

As the company pivots toward electrification, its marketing strategies must evolve to resonate with a new generation of consumers while building on its storied legacy. This dynamic landscape presents both challenges and opportunities, prompting GM to adopt creative and engaging approaches that reflect its commitment to sustainability and innovation.

At the heart of GM's marketing efforts is the realization that consumers are increasingly interested in the stories behind the products they purchase. Today's buyers want to know more than just specifications; they seek a deeper connection to brands that align with their values.

With electric vehicles, this connection is particularly important, as sustainability and environmental consciousness are top of mind for many consumers. GM has responded by crafting narratives that emphasize its dedication to creating a greener future through innovative technology and sustainable practices. One way GM has effectively engaged consumers is by highlighting its advancements in electric vehicle technology.

Through targeted campaigns, the company has showcased its commitment to research and development, emphasizing how its cutting-edge batteries and EV platforms, such as the recently rebranded multi-chemistry strategy, contribute to a more sustainable transportation ecosystem.

By focusing on technological innovation, GM positions itself as a forward-thinking leader in the EV space, appealing to environmentally conscious consumers who value progress and sustainability. GM's marketing strategy has also embraced storytelling through various media channels. From impactful television ads to engaging social media content, the company is leveraging a multi-faceted approach to reach its audience.

By sharing compelling stories of real customers who have made the switch to electric vehicles, GM illustrates the tangible benefits of owning an EV, such as lower operating costs, reduced emissions, and a quieter driving experience.

These relatable narratives help potential buyers envision themselves as part of the EV revolution, making the transition feel not only attainable but desirable. In addition to storytelling, GM has ramped up its presence at major events and initiatives that resonate with its target audience. The company has strategically aligned itself with events focused on sustainability and technology, allowing it to showcase its electric vehicles in environments where like-minded consumers gather.

For instance, participating in environmental expos and tech conferences provides GM with opportunities to engage directly with potential buyers, offering hands-on experiences with its vehicles and fostering meaningful conversations about the future of transportation.

Social media has become a cornerstone of GM's marketing strategy, enabling the company to connect with consumers in real time and foster community engagement. Platforms like Instagram, Twitter, and Facebook allow GM to share updates, answer questions, and celebrate milestones with its audience. By creating interactive content—such as polls, quizzes, and behind-the-scenes glimpses of the manufacturing process—GM encourages consumers to participate in the conversation, making them feel like active contributors to the brand's journey.

This two-way interaction builds trust and loyalty, reinforcing GM's image as a customer-centric company. Moreover, GM has recognized the power of influencer partnerships in reaching new audiences.

By collaborating with influencers who align with the company's values, GM can tap into existing communities of EV enthusiasts and environmentally conscious consumers. These influencers often share authentic experiences with GM's vehicles, amplifying the brand's message and extending its reach to demographics that might not have been engaged through traditional advertising channels. This approach not only enhances brand visibility but also fosters a sense of authenticity and relatability.

As part of its commitment to transparency and education, GM has also focused on demystifying the electric vehicle experience for potential buyers. Many consumers still harbor misconceptions about EVs, such as concerns over range, charging infrastructure, and overall performance.

To address these issues, GM has launched educational campaigns that provide clear, factual information about the benefits of electric vehicles. By simplifying complex topics and answering common questions, GM empowers consumers to make informed decisions about their transportation choices. However, GM's marketing efforts are not without their challenges. The electric vehicle market is highly competitive, with numerous automakers vying for consumer attention.

To stand out, GM must continuously innovate its messaging and branding strategies to remain relevant. This requires an ongoing commitment to understanding consumer preferences and adapting campaigns to meet evolving demands.

Additionally, as the EV market continues to mature, GM must remain vigilant about maintaining its reputation. High-profile marketing campaigns, such as those featuring celebrity endorsements or major sponsorships, can backfire if the company fails to deliver on its promises regarding product quality and performance. Therefore, GM must ensure that its marketing aligns with its product development, creating a seamless experience for consumers from the first impression to the moment they drive off in their new electric vehicle.

GM's marketing and advertising efforts reflect a thoughtful and dynamic approach to engaging consumers in the electric vehicle revolution.

By leveraging storytelling, embracing social media, and fostering community engagement, GM is building meaningful connections with potential buyers while addressing their concerns and aspirations. As the company navigates the evolving landscape of electric mobility, its marketing strategies will play a pivotal role in shaping public perception and driving adoption of electric vehicles.

With a focus on innovation, sustainability, and customer engagement, GM is not just selling cars; it's championing a movement toward a more sustainable future for all.

Chapter Twelve; Rethinking Manufacturing and Production Facilities

As General Motors (GM) continues to navigate the complexities of the electric vehicle (EV) revolution, it is not just the vehicles themselves that are undergoing transformation; the entire manufacturing and production landscape is being reimagined.

This evolution reflects the company's commitment to adaptability, innovation, and sustainability in an industry that is rapidly changing. Rethinking manufacturing and production facilities is not just a strategic necessity for GM; it represents a profound shift in how the company views its role in the automotive ecosystem.

At the core of this transformation is the realization that the traditional manufacturing models used for internal combustion engine vehicles may not be suitable for electric vehicles. The transition to EV production requires different technologies, processes, and skills.

For instance, the production of electric vehicles involves the integration of advanced battery technology, which necessitates a complete rethink of the supply chain, from sourcing materials to assembling the final product. GM recognizes that adapting its manufacturing strategies is essential to maintaining competitiveness and meeting the growing demand for electric vehicles. One significant aspect of this rethinking process involves the design and layout of production facilities.

Traditional automotive plants were optimized for assembly lines focused on internal combustion engines, with processes tailored to those vehicles. In contrast, electric vehicles require more flexible and efficient manufacturing systems that can accommodate various battery chemistries and vehicle architectures.

GM is investing in modernizing its facilities to support these new production methods, incorporating automation and advanced robotics to enhance efficiency and precision. Moreover, the shift toward electric vehicles has prompted GM to reconsider its approach to sustainability within manufacturing. As consumers become increasingly concerned about environmental impacts, automakers are under pressure to reduce their carbon footprints throughout the entire production process.

GM is committed to making its manufacturing operations more sustainable by integrating renewable energy sources, minimizing waste, and optimizing resource use. This not only aligns with consumer values but also positions GM as a leader in the effort to create a greener automotive industry.

In addition to rethinking facility designs, GM is also exploring innovative partnerships and collaborations to enhance its manufacturing capabilities. By working with suppliers, technology firms, and even other automakers, GM aims to leverage external expertise and share best practices in production techniques. This collaborative spirit is crucial for navigating the complexities of EV manufacturing, as it allows GM to stay at the forefront of technological advancements while fostering a culture of innovation within its own operations.

As part of this initiative, GM has already begun to establish dedicated EV production plants. For example, Factory Zero in Detroit represents a state-of-the-art facility specifically designed for electric vehicle assembly.

This plant embodies GM's vision of an eco-friendly manufacturing environment, incorporating sustainable practices and advanced technology to streamline production. By concentrating its resources on dedicated EV facilities, GM can improve efficiency, reduce lead times, and enhance quality control, ultimately delivering better products to consumers. Employee training and development are also critical components of this rethinking process.

As GM transitions to electric vehicle manufacturing, it must ensure that its workforce possesses the skills necessary to adapt to new technologies and processes. This means investing in training programs that equip employees with the knowledge and expertise to work with advanced battery systems and electric drivetrains.

By fostering a culture of continuous learning, GM empowers its workforce to embrace change and thrive in a rapidly evolving industry. Consumer expectations are shifting alongside these manufacturing changes. Today's buyers are more informed and engaged, demanding transparency about how their vehicles are made. In response, GM is committed to open communication about its manufacturing processes and sustainability efforts.

This transparency builds trust with consumers, reinforcing the message that GM is not only producing electric vehicles but doing so in a responsible and ethical manner. While the transition to electric vehicle manufacturing presents numerous opportunities, it also comes with challenges.

The need to balance production capacity with fluctuating demand is a critical concern. GM must remain agile, capable of adjusting its production strategies based on market dynamics while ensuring that its facilities are prepared to meet consumer needs. This adaptability is essential in a landscape where EV adoption rates can vary significantly depending on economic conditions and consumer sentiment. However, GM's rethinking of its manufacturing and production facilities reflects a holistic approach to the electric vehicle revolution.

By modernizing its plants, embracing sustainability, investing in employee training, and fostering collaborations, GM is positioning itself for success in an increasingly competitive market.

This transformation goes beyond the vehicles themselves; it represents a commitment to reshaping the entire manufacturing process to align with the evolving needs of consumers and the planet. As GM continues to innovate and adapt, it is not merely keeping pace with industry changes—it is leading the charge toward a more sustainable and electrifying future for the automotive world.

The road ahead may be challenging, but GM's proactive and forward-thinking strategies pave the way for a new era in manufacturing, one that prioritizes both performance and responsibility.

Chapter Thirteen; Lessons Learned and Future Directions

As General Motors (GM) navigates the ever-evolving landscape of electric vehicles (EVs), it has not only embraced change but also learned valuable lessons from both successes and challenges along the way.

Each step of this journey has provided insights that will shape GM's future direction, allowing it to adapt and innovate in a highly competitive market. Understanding these lessons is crucial, not just for GM, but for the entire automotive industry as it transitions toward a more sustainable future. One of the most significant lessons GM has learned is the importance of flexibility in its operations.

The automotive market has witnessed unprecedented shifts in consumer preferences, regulatory requirements, and technological advancements. GM initially set ambitious production targets for its electric vehicles, anticipating rapid adoption.

However, as the market evolved, it became clear that the transition to EVs would not happen as quickly as some had hoped. This realization prompted GM to rethink its production goals and strategies, emphasizing the need for agility in manufacturing and planning. The ability to pivot in response to market dynamics will be critical as the company continues to develop and refine its electric vehicle offerings. Another key takeaway for GM has been the value of collaboration.

The complexity of EV manufacturing necessitates partnerships across the supply chain. Whether it's working with battery suppliers to secure critical materials or collaborating with technology firms to enhance software capabilities, GM has recognized that no single entity can navigate this transformation alone.

These partnerships foster innovation and help mitigate risks associated with new technologies. By building a robust network of collaborators, GM is positioning itself to stay ahead of industry trends and consumer expectations. Sustainability has also emerged as a central theme in GM's lessons learned. As consumers become increasingly environmentally conscious, the pressure is on automakers to reduce their carbon footprints not only in vehicle emissions but also throughout the production process.

GM has embraced this challenge by implementing sustainable practices in its manufacturing facilities and supply chain. The company is not only focused on producing electric vehicles but is also committed to ensuring that its entire operation reflects a dedication to sustainability.

This holistic approach resonates with consumers who prioritize ethical choices, reinforcing GM's brand image as a forward-thinking leader in the automotive industry. Furthermore, GM has recognized the importance of transparency in its communication with consumers. As the EV market expands, potential buyers are seeking more information about the products they purchase, including details about the sourcing of materials and the environmental impact of manufacturing processes.

GM has taken proactive steps to provide clarity around its sustainability efforts and the technology behind its vehicles. This transparency fosters trust and confidence among consumers, making them more likely to consider GM's electric vehicles as viable options.

Additionally, GM's experience has highlighted the significance of employee engagement and training. As the automotive industry evolves, so too must the skills of the workforce. GM is committed to investing in its employees, equipping them with the knowledge and training needed to excel in an electrified future. This investment not only enhances the company's production capabilities but also boosts morale and fosters a culture of innovation. When employees feel valued and empowered, they are more likely to contribute creative ideas and solutions, driving the company forward.

Looking to the future, GM is committed to refining its strategies based on these lessons. The company understands that the path to electrification is not a sprint but a marathon, requiring patience, resilience, and ongoing adaptation.

As GM continues to innovate, it will prioritize the development of diverse battery chemistries, improved charging infrastructure, and advanced technologies that enhance the overall EV experience for consumers. This includes exploring new manufacturing techniques that increase efficiency while reducing costs. Moreover, GM recognizes the need to expand its electric vehicle portfolio to meet the diverse needs of consumers. While the focus has been on high-performance models, GM understands that a wider range of affordable options is essential for broader market acceptance.

By investing in research and development, GM aims to create electric vehicles that cater to various segments of the market, making the transition to electrification more accessible to all consumers.

The company's commitment to community engagement will also play a crucial role in its future direction. GM recognizes that building relationships with local communities is essential for fostering acceptance and enthusiasm for electric vehicles. Through outreach initiatives, partnerships with local organizations, and educational programs, GM aims to inform and inspire consumers about the benefits of EVs. This grassroots approach will help cultivate a supportive environment for the growth of electric vehicle adoption.

Moreover, the lessons GM has learned through its journey in the electric vehicle market will undoubtedly shape its future directions. By embracing flexibility, fostering collaboration, prioritizing sustainability, and investing in its workforce, GM is well-equipped to navigate the challenges and opportunities that lie ahead.

As the company continues to innovate and adapt, it remains committed to leading the charge toward a more sustainable future for the automotive industry. With each lesson learned, GM is not only evolving as a manufacturer but also positioning itself as a trusted partner in the global movement toward electrification. The road ahead may be uncertain, but GM's dedication to progress and responsibility will guide its journey into the future.

Chapter Fourteen; Current and Future EV Production Plants

As General Motors (GM) accelerates its transition to electric vehicles (EVs), the development and optimization of production plants stand at the forefront of its strategy.

These facilities are not merely assembly lines; they represent a commitment to innovation, sustainability, and a vision for the future of mobility. GM's current and future EV production plants reflect the company's dedication to meeting the evolving demands of the automotive market while also embracing the principles of responsible manufacturing.

One of GM's flagship EV production facilities is Factory Zero in Detroit, which symbolizes the company's shift toward electric mobility. Factory Zero is a state-of-the-art facility designed specifically for the assembly of electric vehicles.

The name itself speaks volumes about GM's vision: a factory that is zero-emissions and fully committed to sustainable practices. This plant embodies GM's goal of not only producing electric vehicles but doing so in a way that minimizes environmental impact. The facility integrates advanced manufacturing technologies, including automation and robotics, to enhance efficiency while reducing waste.

The decision to establish Factory Zero was driven by a growing recognition that the traditional automotive manufacturing model needed to evolve. The facility is designed to support the assembly of multiple EV models, allowing GM to pivot quickly as market demands change.

This flexibility is crucial as the automotive landscape continues to shift toward electrification. By centralizing EV production in a facility equipped with the latest technologies, GM can streamline its operations and respond effectively to consumer preferences. Looking to the future, GM has ambitious plans to expand its network of EV production plants. The company is in the process of developing additional facilities that will further enhance its manufacturing capabilities.

These future plants will be designed with sustainability in mind, incorporating renewable energy sources and efficient manufacturing practices to minimize carbon emissions. As GM aims to achieve carbon neutrality by 2040, these new plants will play a vital role in that journey.

A key aspect of GM's future production strategy is the diversification of battery technologies. The company is moving toward a multi-chemistry battery strategy, which allows for greater flexibility in sourcing materials and adapting to market needs. This means that GM's future plants will be equipped to produce various battery types, optimizing performance for different vehicle models. This strategic shift not only improves efficiency but also positions GM to be a leader in battery technology, a crucial component of the EV ecosystem.

GM's investment in new production facilities is not limited to North America. The company is also exploring opportunities for expansion in international markets. Establishing plants in different regions allows GM to tap into local resources, labor, and consumer bases.

This global approach to production aligns with the company's vision of being a major player in the worldwide electric vehicle market, catering to the unique needs of diverse markets while ensuring the same high standards of quality and sustainability across the board. A noteworthy aspect of GM's future production plants is the emphasis on community engagement. As the company expands its manufacturing footprint, it recognizes the importance of building positive relationships with local communities.

GM is committed to creating jobs, investing in workforce training, and supporting local economies in the areas where its plants are located. By engaging with communities, GM aims to foster goodwill and support for its electric vehicle initiatives, ensuring that the transition to EVs is a collaborative effort.

The company is also keenly aware of the challenges it faces in ramping up production. Supply chain disruptions, material shortages, and fluctuating demand can pose significant hurdles in the automotive industry. GM is addressing these challenges head-on by strengthening its relationships with suppliers and investing in supply chain resilience. By diversifying its supplier base and exploring alternative materials for battery production, GM aims to mitigate risks and ensure a steady flow of components for its future plants.

As GM continues to innovate in its production processes, employee training and development remain a priority. The transition to electric vehicle production requires a workforce equipped with new skills and knowledge.

GM is committed to investing in its employees, providing training programs that focus on the technologies and processes involved in EV manufacturing. By empowering its workforce, GM is not only enhancing its production capabilities but also fostering a culture of innovation and adaptability. In summary, GM's current and future EV production plants represent a pivotal component of its strategy to lead in the electric vehicle market. Through facilities like Factory Zero, the company is demonstrating its commitment to sustainable manufacturing practices and innovative technologies.

As GM expands its production capabilities, it remains focused on flexibility, community engagement, and workforce development, ensuring that it is well-positioned to meet the demands of an electrified future.

The journey toward a sustainable automotive industry is filled with challenges, but GM's proactive approach to developing its production plants is a testament to its dedication to shaping a better, more sustainable future for all. As these plants come online, they will not only produce vehicles but also serve as beacons of progress in the evolving landscape of the automotive industry.

Conclusion

In conclusion, this book has taken you on an insightful journey through the transformative landscape of General Motors' electric vehicle strategy.

As we navigated the challenges and triumphs of the company, it became evident that GM is not merely adapting to a changing market; it is redefining what it means to be a leader in the automotive industry. From the decision to drop the "Ultium" name to the ambitious production goals and the shift toward diverse battery chemistries, GM's commitment to innovation and sustainability shines through every aspect of its strategy.

The automotive industry is at a pivotal moment, and GM is positioning itself at the forefront of this evolution. The company's forward-thinking approach is exemplified by its investments in state-of-the-art production facilities and its focus on community engagement.

As we discussed, the success of GM's electric vehicle initiatives is deeply intertwined with its ability to adapt to market conditions and embrace new technologies. The lessons learned along this journey emphasize the importance of flexibility, collaboration, and a commitment to sustainable practices. Moreover, GM's emphasis on employee training and development reflects its understanding that the workforce is vital to the realization of its vision.

By investing in its employees, GM is not only enhancing its production capabilities but also fostering a culture of innovation and resilience that will serve the company well in the years to come. As we look toward the future, it is clear that the road ahead will be filled with both challenges and opportunities.

GM's commitment to carbon neutrality and its dedication to producing a diverse range of electric vehicles will play a significant role in shaping the future of transportation. The company's journey is a testament to the belief that with determination and innovation, we can create a more sustainable and efficient automotive landscape. I want to take this opportunity to thank you, the readers, for your time and interest in this book.

Your engagement with GM's journey reflects a shared commitment to understanding and supporting the transition to electric mobility. Together, we can embrace the exciting possibilities that lie ahead and contribute to a brighter, more sustainable future in the automotive industry. Thank you for being a part of this exploration.

www.ingramcontent.com/pod-product-compliance
Lightning Source LLC
Chambersburg PA
CBHW050306230526
45471CB00005B/2052